100 Things DURAN DURAN FANS Should Know & Do During This Life

ALSO BY SANDY LENDER

The *Choices* Series
Choices Meant for Gods
Choices Meant for Kings
Choices Meant for All

The *Dragons in Space* Series
Problems on Eldora Prime
Problems Above Pangaea Moon
Problems in Annady's Core

The *Faerie Holidays* Series
May Your Heart Be Light
My Faerie Valentine
I Know What Your Vampire Did Last Summer
Have Yourself a Faerie Little Christmas

Award-winning Poetry
Poems of Trials, Triumphs, and Turtles
Poems of Fact, Form, and Fantasy

And more...

100 Things
DURAN DURAN FANS
Should Know & Do
During This Life

a new, quirky guide to nostalgia
from 1978 to Danse Macabre

SANDY LENDER

IYF Publishing/Dragon Hoard Press

100 Things Duran Duran Fans Should Know & Do During This Life: a new, quirky guide to nostalgia from 1978 to Danse Macabre is a non-fiction work prepared by the international best-seller, award-winning author Sandy Lender without the use of AI.

The font used for the interior of this book is Montserrat. Duranies know why.
(I've also used 12-point size for the majority of the text to accommodate our aging Duranie eyes.)

Cover design by Sandy Lender without the use of AI
Edited by Jen Selinsky

ISBN: 978-1-7378129-6-8
www.SandyLenderInk.com
Printed in the United States of America

Dedication

Could there be any doubt?

To Taylor, Rhodes, Le Bon

...and the supporting artists
who collaborated with the band
to make the soundtrack to my life...

Acknowledgments

First and foremost, I want to thank my personal Lord and Savior Jesus Christ, who keeps me reaching up for the sunrise each day and filled with hope that there's something better awaiting me after this life. While I'm here, I thank every friend who has sung along and danced with me at a show. My biggest thanks goes to those friends who have shared those experiences and facilitated getting to the shows during dark times.

The best stories begin with, "Christine, Jennine, and I were in (insert name of a city here)." It would fill half this book to list all my DD friends, and I'm afraid of missing anyone, so let me assure you—Christine, Jennine, Laura, Larry & Joel, Shannon and Trish who snuck the Walkman to me in the eighties, Sunshine the deejay, Dianne, Robyn, Jen, the Florida Duranies group, Ginger, Aluska, Megan who filled the gap in Tampa, Andy, and many more people—you are important and valued in my musical life.

Thank you for hanging out with me.

Thank you for sending happy emojis for the random DD texts I fling at you.

Thank you for helping me hobble out of concert halls, or off the festival lot, in my bad shoes.

Introduction

Let me admit, up front, you're about to read a frivolous romp through a Duranie's brain. We're about to dance together down Memory Lane, inspired by a *Star Wars* book title I saw about three or four months ago. To prevent myself from stealing the author's intellectual property, I didn't open the unauthorized *100 Things Star Wars Fans Should Know & Do Before They Die.*

Instead, I've put together a Duran-o-rama of my own making. It's arranged exactly as the title suggests: first an item of what a Duran Duran fan should know, followed by an item a fan can do. This order proceeds from one to one hundred in a conversational tone.

The prompts of nostalgia might be numbered, but they're not in chronological order. Most of the to-do items are geared toward sharing your insanity with others. Basically, you're holding amusing reminders of carefree times when a ticket to a concert cost all of eighteen dollars, when you listened to the local radio station at midnight because they were playing the entire new DD release, or when you could grab a crew of giggling girls to plop down on the couch with a six-pack of Pepsi—because that's what John preferred over the sponsor of the *Arena* tour—to watch and sing along to *Arena: An Absurd Notion*, complete with parental advisory.

Now, let me lift the needle off the record for a second.

That parental advisory brings me to the elephant in the room, which I must address. It would be disingenuous of me to write an "all the things Duranies should do" book without admitting I didn't do most of these things until after the 1980s, including the viewing of *Arena*. At least until after 1988, when I went to college.

My entrance to teenagerhood in 1983 came with a side of parental paranoia. My folks were concerned my burgeoning obsession with DD was unhealthy. Rather than seeing it as harmless Beatlemania transferred to Duran-mania, they saw it as something to be silenced, and for my own good, they forbade me to listen to music.*

My record player, boombox, cassette tapes, 45s, teeny bopper magazines, band posters, and other musical paraphernalia were removed from my room or destroyed. That was during the mid-1980s, when, for some bizarre reason, we weren't allowed to have Sony Walkmans at my public high school, so the red cassette player a friend snuck into my oversize coat pocket had to be carefully concealed from school officials, bus drivers, parents, and a younger sister whom I'm pretty sure was getting paid to rat me out. My telephone calls were limited to ten minutes at a time and monitored in the kitchen, and my television viewing was similarly monitored. There was no MTV, *Friday Night Videos*, or *Miami Vice* in my house—I didn't see the episode with The Power Station's cameo until adulthood, after it was uploaded to YouTube.

Reader, that was around the age when I learned to be a secret agent! The immediate, easy, and only thing I accomplished on the day of The Great Purge was throwing a black-and-white photo of John Taylor I was using as a bookmark into *The Turquoise Mask* by Phyllis A. Whitney and taking that with me to the living room while my bedroom was decimated. I could have filled several of the to-do items in this book with ways to surreptitiously move DD contraband from one locale to the next. For example, while it's almost cliché, it's absolutely possible to hide a cassette tape in a hollowed-out book. Here are a couple tips:

- It's gotta be a hardcover.
- It's gotta be thick enough for the cassette (or CD or DVD) you wish to hide.
- You want to take the trash with you to your next location to dispose of it. Put that in your pocket/bookbag and throw it away off-site.

Now, in most "troubled" homes, kids were hiding alcohol, cigarettes, condoms, or drugs from their parents. Not me. I was sneaking music playing devices around so I could listen to the moody intro of "New Religion" through headphones on a foggy walk to the bus stop at the top of the street.

I tell you this so you understand my enthusiasm for all things Duran isn't just a passing phase. I've been into the group and their music since I heard "New Moon on Monday" in junior high. My vinyl DD collection is why I still own a turntable, and my CD DD collection fills three shelves of a thirty-two-inch-wide CD bookcase. I've traveled to DD conventions with friends, and if I could've confirmed any of those events still exist, I'd have included attending one in the to-do list of this book. I lost track of how many DD and Duran-adjacent shows (like Neurotic Outsiders) I'd attended after thirty of them and stopped trying to track them all. Now, when people ask how many concerts I've been to, my response of, "It's over thirty" freaks them out enough, a real number is probably unnecessary.

Another item I'm going to mark as unnecessary is telling you all the basics in the "to know" portions of this book. I mean, if you've picked up this book, then you probably know Duran Duran is a supergroup out of Birmingham, England from the eighties, and the original Fab Five are John Taylor, Nick Rhodes, Simon Le Bon, Roger Taylor, and Andy Taylor. You'd have to be living under a rock to have missed the announcement of Andy's battle against prostate cancer at the Rock & Roll Hall of Fame induction ceremony. There are facts and stats that fill biographies at your local bookstore. (I uploaded a review of Jen Selinsky's *Reach Up for the Sunrise*, published by Wymer UK Publishing, on my BookTube channel on September 26, 2021.) There are a multitude of great interviews conducted during every album release junket. I highly recommend the *Future Past* marketing interviews to see the energy and camaraderie among the band. They're a pleasure to experience! And I highly recommend sitting back with a Pepsi or your favorite wine to revel in the absurd notion of *100 Things Duran Duran Fans Should Know & Do During This Life*.

Enjoy this random compilation of fun frivolity from a fellow Duranie's brain. It's a joy to be in this fandom with you!

With love and music,
Sandy Lender

**I must be transparent and share that my folks recognized the historic significance of the Live-Aid, all-day, around-the-world concert that took place in 1985 to raise funds for starving humans in Africa, and I was allowed to watch that. I was devastated when my bedtime came before DD took the stage and I missed their live performance. However, of course, I've watched it on replays.*

100 Things Duran Duran Fans Should Know & Do During This Life

1. Is There Something I Should Know?

Song Abbreviations

Duranies—and random journalists, I've noticed—abbreviate the titles of the band's songs as a sort of shorthand. "A View to a Kill" is AVTAK. "Girls on Film" is GOF.

I must admit, the acronyms catch me off guard sometimes and I'll stare at a computer screen for a few minutes before I realize a fellow Duranie didn't capitalize the abbreviation for "Michael You've Got a Lot to Answer For."

Throughout this book, the entries for things Duran Duran fans should know will be preceded with ITSISK, which you've probably figured out is the acronym for the song "Is There Something I Should Know," from the 1983 Capitol release of the band's first album.

Considering the wide array of humans who might grab this book off the shelf, I don't want to exclude anyone from the club, so I'll refrain from abbreviating *all* the song titles throughout.

I want to cater to all the fan levels and welcome everyone in.

2. To Do

Ignore the haters.

Being a Duranie has made me a source of ridicule for most of my life. Since 1984 when I heard "New Moon on Monday" and became a fan, bullies have made fun of me for my exuberance and snobs have looked down on me for my musical preferences. Forty years is a long time to endure strangers (and some acquaintances) mocking you for something you love and enjoy, but it helps you grow a thick skin. It also helps you learn to ignore bullies and haters in other areas of life.

I encourage you to do the same if you find someone laughing at you because they don't "get" the genius behind a supergroup that's been making music since 1978.

I encourage you to find your Duranie tribe and enjoy the amusing ideas in this book.

3. ITSISK

The ragged tiger from DD's third studio album, *Seven and the Ragged Tiger*, stands for success.

4. To Do

Appreciate the band.

Every August 10 is National Duran Duran Appreciation Day. Yes, it's a thing. Yes, we Duranies celebrate with music, cake, libations, texting one another, posting pictures of ourselves in full DD regalia on social media, and more. Typically, at least one member of the band posts a message to the fans on that day as well, acknowledging we're all out here making the most of our zany fandom.

5. ITSISK

Naming Conventions

The villain from the 1968 science fiction movie *Barbarella*, from which the band gets its name, spells his name Durand Durand. Personally, I'm thankful John and Nick dropped the extra ds.

6. To Do

Mark the new moons.

Even if it's not the turning of the year when you pick up this book, you can tackle this to-do whenever you think of it. Go through your calendar and mark the new moons that occur on Mondays. Those are *defacto* holidays for Duranies, and you don't want them to slip by without notice.

On a Monday with a new moon, you want to listen to at least "New Moon on Monday," if not the entire *Seven and the Ragged Tiger* album. You also want to text all your Duranie friends with Happy New Moon on Monday messages. Some years, we only get one of these, so treat it like the holiday it is!

7. ITSISK

A bit more on naming concepts

One of the names John and Nick considered for the band during the early days was RAF, which stands for Royal Air Force. You can see that idea in the "militaristic" retro garb they wore at the Rum Runner photo shoots, and of course, in the video for "Is There Something I Should Know."

8. To Do

Go see the band live.

This one's kind of obvious. Make a plan to attend one of the band's concerts, if you haven't already. (Even if you have, plan to attend another.)

Seeing DD live is a fantastic experience. If you haven't seen them live and only listened to them on the radio or on pre-recorded media, you'll be stunned by how hard "The Wild Boys," "Careless Memories," "White Lines," "New Religion," "Hallucinating Elvis," "Too Much Information," or any number of their awesome songs can rock out.

Please note, the audience at a DD show is a bit different than an audience at a festival or multi-artist event, so entry number eight is specifically about finding a DD concert where the band is the main event. At that show, they're playing a wider variety from their catalogue to entertain and please the fan base in attendance, and they'll likely be on the stage for a longer time than they would at a festival. (You understand that concept.)

9. ITSISK

Simon's Intro

Simon's ex-girlfriend, Fiona Kemp, was working as a waitress in a cocktail bar, that much is true...

To be serious, Fiona was working at the Rum Runner when the members of DD were auditioning singers. She contacted her former boyfriend, Simon Le Bon, to turn him on to the opportunity.

Thank you, Fiona, wherever you are today!

10. To Do

See the band at a festival.

This one's a spin-off of number eight. Make a plan to attend one of the band's shows at a festival or multiple-artist event, if you haven't already.

Seeing DD perform and surprise the crap out of people who may not be rabid fans or who might not have seen them live before, is a fun experience.

Please note, the audience at a festival isn't going to be wall-to-wall (or fence-to-fence) Duranies. Be ready for the negative people who are there to see other bands or who came with a

Duranie because they had no choice. I can remember the surprising and horrible experience of a crowd in Denver booing when the band had to stop and wait for stagehands to fix a technical issue that was screwing with the sound. The band had to wait, patiently, while the potheads in the audience booed and acted like spoiled brats. When the issue was resolved and the techs left the stage, DD resumed the show, and it rocked.

At that type of show, they're playing a smaller variety from their catalogue to entertain the people who have only heard them on the radio and who wouldn't know a B-side if it slapped them in the face, and they'll likely be on the stage for a shorter time than they would at their own event. (You understand that concept.)

11. ITSISK

DD Front Men

Simon John Charles Le Bon is not the first front man for DD. The singers who came before him include:

- Stephen Duffy
- Andy Wickett
- Jeff Thomas.

In some biographies, you hear tell of Simon Colley (who played clarinet and bass during the early days), serving on the mic.

12. To Do
Mark the birthdays.

Each member of the band should have his birthday celebrated, of course. "It's Roger's birthday," is a great excuse to give for listening nonstop to the band's music for twenty-four hours, right? Here's your list of days to host a party or just stream DD videos with zero guilt, in calendar-year order:

February 16—Andy Taylor
April 26—Roger Taylor
May 3—Sterling Campbell
June 8—Nick Rhodes
June 14—Dom Brown
June 20—John Taylor
October 27—Simon Le Bon
December 8—Warren Cuccurullo

13. ITSISK
Nick!

Nick Rhodes is the backbone of the band. As one of the founding members, he has remained at the helm—at the controls, if you will—unwavering since the beginning in 1978.

14. To Do
Read it for fun.

Rob Sheffield wrote a self-indulgent romp (not quite like this one) called *Talking to Girls About Duran Duran: One Young Man's Quest for True Love and a Cooler Haircut* that will take you on a nostalgic dance down Memory Lane if you experienced the eighties first-hand.

The title is deceptive, although the narrative is bookended with DD and laced with musical references. It's enjoyable, for sure. The hardcover was released in 2010 from Plume, an imprint of Penguin; the paperback is available, as well.

15. ITSISK

Simon's Accolades

Simon Le Bon has won (as of this printing) three Ivor Novello awards as well as two Grammy awards and two MTV Music awards. He has also received a Silver Clef award and an ASCAP Golden Note award. Most recently, he's been appointed a Member of the Order of the British Empire (MBE) for his service in charity and music.

16. To Do

Read it for too much information.

Prolific, award-winning author and fellow Duranie, Jen Selinsky, wrote a band biography filled with facts and stats for the new Duranie. Published by Wymer UK Publishing in July 2021, *Reach Up for The Sunrise: A Duran Duran Biography*, details the history of the band right up to the *Future Past* release. It's available in both paperback and electronic formats. Jen has also written three other Duran-related books:

- *Rio: Poems Inspired by Duran Duran*;
- *Careless Memories: More Works Inspired by Duran Duran*; and
- *Hungry Like the Wolf: Duran Duran and My Life*.

The books are available on Amazon and other online book retailers.

Music journalist, Lyndsey Parker, also released an e-book called *Careless Memories of Strange Behavior: My Notorious Life as a Duran Duran Fan – A Single Notes Book*. Though the book is only available in e-format, it's from a great perspective of one Duranie to another. Lyndsey talks about her DD fandom during her teenage years. The book is available on Amazon.

In 2017, Morgan Richter released *Duranalysis: essays on the duran duran experience*. It's a paperback collection of essays on our fave band. The book is also available on Amazon.

Superfan Andrew "Durandy" Golub has a handful of DD-related books including a hefty, gorgeous, full-color coffee table book titled *Beautiful Colors: The Posters of Duran Duran* with a foreword by Nick Rhodes. The hardcover full of glossy pages is available directly from Andy when you reach out to him at contact@durandy.com.

Basically, the desire for DD information didn't end with the eighties, and Duranies still produce and consume all forms of media about the band. It's out there for you to enjoy!

17. ITSISK

Waiting for the Night Boat

"Night Boat" was the first song DD played live together with the official lineup of Simon, John, Nick, Roger, and Andy. (Source: John Taylor's *In the Pleasure Groove*)

18. To Do

Read it for official, real talk.

John took matters into his own hands and worked with biographer/writer Tom Sykes to prepare the book, *In the Pleasure Groove: Love, Death & Duran Duran,* released by Dutton, a member of Penguin Group, in 2012.

I can't recommend the book highly enough, for John's dry wit and first-hand account of how it all went down. The book is available on Amazon and other online book retailers.

19. ITSISK

Song Cameos

A View to a Kill isn't the only movie to use a DD song. "Notorious" has a cameo in the 2001 movie *Donnie Darko* when the grade-school girls do their dance routine to the peppy song.

"Do You Believe in Shame?" is used in *Tequila Sunrise* (and Andy Taylor's "Dead on the Money" appears on the soundtrack as well). "Hungry Like the Wolf" was featured in six films (so far), including 2003's *Old School* and 1984's *Hot Dog...the Movie*. There are more out there to watch and listen for!

20. To Do

Marathon the albums.

Aww, Sandy, listening to all those albums will take forever!

Yes. Yes, it will. And it will be fabulous.

Start with *Duran Duran* from 1981 (or with The Devils' *Dark Circles*, released in 2002 but written and originally "worked" during the band's early days) and listen your way all the way through the albums to and through *Danse Macabre*.

I'll list them for you in the next item as something you should know.

21. ITSISK

Band Discography

You should definitely know the discography.

Because it would fill multiple pages to list out all the singles, EPs, demos, remixes, re-releases, and videos, let's focus on full-length albums.

[*Dark Circles*, by The Devils, released in 2002]
Duran Duran (1981) (again in 1983)
Rio (1982)
Seven and the Ragged Tiger (1983)
[*Arena*, while not a studio album, 1984]
[*The Power Station 33 1/3*, by The Power Station, 1985]
[*So Red the Rose*, by Arcadia, 1985]
Notorious (1986)
Big Thing (1988)
[*Decade*, a compilation album, 1989]
Liberty (1990)
Duran Duran (aka. *The Wedding Album*) (1993)
[*Thank You*, a covers album, 1995]
Medazzaland (1997)
[*Night Versions*, a remixes compilation album, 1998]
[*Greatest*, a compilation album, 1998]
[*Strange Behaviour*, a remixes compilation album, 1999]
Pop Trash (2000)
[*The Singles Boxset 1*, 2003]
[*The Singles Boxset 2*, 2004]
Astronaut (2004)
Red Carpet Massacre (2007)
All You Need Is Now (2011)
A Diamond in the Mind: Live (2012)
Paper Gods (2015)
Future Past (2021)
Danse Macabre (2023)

22. To Do

Frame it.

If you're one of those folks who no longer has a turntable—and isn't it a shame we let those go?—but you still have your favorite DD album on vinyl, you can get artistic with that thing.

Frame it.

Craft stores, like Hobby Lobby, sell not-too-pricy square frames a vinyl album cover (with disc inside) fit into perfectly. I have "New Moon on Monday" and John Taylor's "I Do What I Do" from *9 ½ Weeks* framed and hanging on the wall as gorgeous art.

23. ITSISK

The music is the power.

During the mid-eighties, John and Andy worked with Bernard Edwards, Tony Thompson, Robert Palmer, and others on a project they dubbed The Power Station. Roger also did some drum work for them. What began as a cover of T-Rex's 1971 hit, "Bang a Gong (Get It On)," turned into an edgier and more rock-oriented group of songs than the typical DD fare.

The supergroup brought in Michael Des Barres when Robert didn't wish to tour. Des Barres took the project on the road in 1985.

24. To Do
Craft it.

Another way to repurpose your old twelve-inch single is to make something out of it.

There are Etsy crafters who will take your vinyl and cut it precisely to fashion a cute little handbag. While there's something about breaking and cutting apart a vinyl album that hurts my soul, I see the creativity in repurposing an album that is slightly damaged or has difficulty being played. It's a startling fashion statement, for sure.

25. ITSISK
Arcadia

In the mid-eighties, while John and Andy worked on The Power Station project, Simon, Nick, and Roger worked on the Arcadia project, producing one of the most beautiful musical masterpieces known to mankind. The album *So Red the Rose* includes guest appearances by Grace Jones, Sting, Roger Waters, and other musicians who increased the moodiness and musical genius of the project.

26. To Do
Be moody and restless.

Another to-do item that should cost close-to-nothing is to listen to *So Red the Rose* by candlelight. I highly recommend listening to the album on a turntable, if possible. However you manage it, dimming the lights and channeling the sound through headphones while you enjoy a glass of Merlot heightens the experience of the masterpiece.

27. ITSISK

You should know your seaside alarms.

On the title track of *Danse Macabre,* Simon convinced the others to use an old recording of the foghorn called the Hawsker Mad Bull.

28. To Do

Gotta catch 'em all!

Catch or collect, we Duranies tend to obsess over having all the things. Do you have a favorite medium for experiencing your music? Do you prefer twelve-inch singles over CD singles? During the 1990s, I discovered the three-inch CD single and decided I needed to collect as many of those as DD would release. They didn't seem to catch on in the music world, but I have a handful that I treasure. Maybe you have a favorite DD song of which you need to have every remix and reissue. From the 45 to the twelve-inch to the "cassingle" and onward...

29. ITSISK

They did it first.

DD was the first—and so far only—band to take a James Bond theme song to the top of the charts, scoring a number one hit with "A View to a Kill."

30. To Do

Curate a playlist.

Pick out your favorite medium and/or service and build a DD-centric playlist with all your favorite DD songs in an order that pleases your soul. Let it gradually build in tempo or let it flow like a bell curve of excitement that fades into something slow and soulful, like "Someone Else Not Me."

31. ITSISK

They did it first.

DD was the first mainstream band to make a song available for digital purchase with "Electric Barbarella."

32. To Do

Write it down, but maybe don't publish it.

Many Duranies have found a creative outlet in writing fanfiction over the years. There are topic threads on the official DD fan message boards where fans can write short stories for one another. While many of those are frivolous, fun outlets for creative dreamscapes, some of them showcase pretty darn good writing chops.

A 2024 debacle titled *Roughing the Princess,* by an author with the pen name Ivy Smoak, reveals why fanfiction shouldn't go to press. But writing a story where your favorite band members inspire a hero or two can be cathartic. It doesn't have to be the oddity Smoak prepared and launched into the world, allegedly embarrassing a female pop icon and football player. Instead, your journaling, poetry, short fiction, or what have you could be a form of writing therapy.

33. ITSISK

They did it first.

DD was the first band to use all Flash animation for a music video with "Someone Else Not Me."

34. To Do

Dig the artwork.

In addition to the creative writing of Duranfanfic you can find—and even participate in—online, there are copious artists who have incredible skill when it comes to illustrating, sketching, or painting the members of the band. Over the years, I've seen some fantastic renderings of band members and it's worth typing keywords along the lines of "illustrations of Duran's John Taylor" into a search engine to find those diamonds in the rough. (Artists on Etsy will even sell that stuff to you if you have that kind of money.)

35. ITSISK

They did it first.

DD was the first band to release a music video completely generated by an artificial intelligence, Huxley, with their song "Invisible" prior to the release of the *Future Past* album. While I'm not a fan of using AI to replace artists or creativity, I applaud the members of the band for breaking ground and sharing their knowledge.

36. To Do

Find a pen pal to share the music between us.

Remember the old days of *Star Hits* and *Tiger Beat* magazines? In the classified ads at the back of many teeny bopper magazines, you could often find one-inch, one-column ads placed by people from all around the world. They were folks who loved a specific type of music, a specific band, a specific genre of literature, and so on, who just wanted to exchange letters—real, written-out-by-hand-on-paper-letters—with other people who had similar interests.

Man, those were the days when people were so much more inclusive and kind. You could send a letter to a person in Finland saying you loved DD's new song and were looking forward to the premier of the new video, and the person in Finland would write back giving their excited impression of the song and video from there.

Lovely, simple friendships were forged over music and common interests.

I encourage you to do that today, but with our more modern—and weeks faster—method of groups on a social media platform. There are plenty of platforms where you can pop in and say, "Hi, I'm a Duranie looking for another Duranie to nerd out with online."

The sad thing about today's society is the preponderance of online trolls who also frequent those groups for the purpose of being rude; but they're easily blocked and ignored. Look for the like-minded humans who want to talk about music, videos, excitement, positivity, fun, and good old-fashioned friendship. I believe they're out there. I believe they used to place ads in the back of *Smash Hits* Magazine...

37. ITSISK

Reportage

Every Duranie knows the band was working on an album between *Astronaut* and the second departure of Andy Taylor. Every Duranie knows that album of songs is sitting somewhere, waiting. As of the printing of this book, Andy Taylor has told the staff at *Classic Pop* Magazine he will complete his parts on the songs that would have appeared on the album *Reportage*. Duranies are waiting for reports of that project.

38. To Do

Play the boardgame.

Back in 1985, the Milton Bradley Company of Springfield, Massachusetts, released a boardgame called Into the Arena. With that game, players collected record, video, and band member cards/tiles from pre-*Notorious* days. It's a collector's item now but still a fun thing to play if you have a drink in one hand and good friends around the table.

39. ITSISK

Duran Time...

If you've been to many DD shows, signings, or special events, you might have heard fellow fans in the lines—or in the concert hall—discussing how many activities they could still sprint to the restroom or bar or merchandise counter to take care of prior to the main event. That was possible because of a phenomenon they called "being on Duran time." It is the acknowledgement that the members of the band, as a group, are not always punctual.

That point is not an admonishment.

The tardiness has become something we fans are accustomed to; some of us find it endearing. If you heard the show starts at 8:00 p.m., no, it doesn't. There's time to run around visiting with friends in the amphitheater.

And that's a wonderful use of Duran time.

40. To Do

Collect the cards.

Back in 1985, Topps® Chewing Gum, Inc., released a set of collector's cards. Each pack had three super-gloss photo cards, three stickers, and a stick of Bazooka® bubble gum (complete with a four-color comic).

The peel-off stickers were of either a band member from the *Arena* tour or a group shot of some assemblage of the band from the tour and promotional spots. On the back of each sticker card was a piece of an image that would make up a mini poster once all fifteen cards of that "set" were collected. On the back of each glossy photo card was a bit of trivia.

Ever since the early days, fans have arranged those cards in a wide array of creative displays. The most interesting I ever saw was one young woman wearing the cards as a dress. Yes, the gal had laminated the cards and chained them together to create a somewhat cylindrical, two-paneled dress, which she wore to a few of the shows in Florida. (At least, that's where I remember seeing her. She might have worn the dress all over the country.)

For this to-do item, see if you can find your set of Duran Duran Topps cards, or see if you can find a set for sale at a DD convention.

41. ITSISK

Rio Revelations

Artist Patrick Nagel painted the iconic woman for the *Rio* album cover and as this book was being prepared for press, word broke that his inspiration for the image had been found.

Popular music news sites credited the Instagram account "@nagel_angel" for the hard work of identifying the image of model Marcie Dinkel—then known as Marcie Hunt. Of course, we no longer have Patrick to confirm the idea, but his assistant Barry Hahn verified Marcie's photo as the foundation for Patrick's painting, according to smoothradio.com.

42. To Do

Host a listening party.

While listening parties typically promote a new release and take place around midnight (or earlier in the evening) before an album's drop, Duranies don't always have that level of patience. We'll put together a listening party for an album that's been out for the past two decades as an excuse to have all our Duranie friends gathered under a theme. It's fantastic to have a *Notorious*-themed party, complete with flaky-bandit costumes.

43. ITSISK

Simon's on the cyber waves.

While everyone and their brother has a podcast these days, Simon Le Bon started one with DD publicist/assistant, Katy Krassner, in 2020. As of this printing, it's still going strong.

The radio program, titled WHOOOSH!, is hosted on The Spectrum channel 28 on SiriusXM each Sunday at 7:00 p.m. EST and Monday at 10:00 p.m. EST. It allows Simon to bring new artists to the forefront while waxing philosophical about music and other creative ideas. Check it out at https://whoooshradio.com/.

44. To Do

Have a Duranoween party.

During my college years, my BFF and I began a tradition near Halloween of celebrating Simon Le Bon's birthday with a DD-themed "party." The first of those was merely the two of us, a VCR with VHS tapes of DD videos, and plenty of cassette tapes.*

**That was during the autumn of 1990 or '91, so the VCR was still the popular way to consume videos.*

As the years progressed, I hosted the annual Simon Le Bon birthday and DD Halloween party at my apartment and later my house in Kansas City. Many Duranies joined us, and my garage was often turned into a disco for the event. Now that DD has released an entire album of thirteen songs devoted to the holiday, fans everywhere can go all in on the idea. Host your own Duranoween in celebration of Simon's birthday plus our obsession.

45. ITSISK

It's based on a real event.

The incredible song, "Sin of the City," from the *Liberty* album references a real, tragic event. On March 25, 1990, a New York City hotspot called Happy Land Club burned down, resulting in the deaths of what newspapers said was eighty-seven people. The song states eighty-nine died, which could be Simon's poetic license to get the syllables and rhyme to work. The discrepancy doesn't change the quality of the song with its important social message.

46. To Do

Isolate the bass.

Not everyone out there recognizes the musical prowess of John Taylor until they listen to one of his isolated bass tracks. It's almost cliché to select "Hold Back the Rain," "Rio," or "Hungry Like the Wolf," at this point (and to marvel at the fact the man was a mere twenty-one years old when he composed those lines), but I also recommend watching one of John's YouTube tutorials from 2020 in which he breaks down the bass lines of a few iconic DD tunes. Each one is a sonic treat.

47. ITSISK

Record Sales

To date, DD has sold over 100 million copies of their albums.

48. To Do

Under the black moonlight...

Here's something that costs zero dollars to do. By the light of the moon, put on the headphones and crank (comfortably loud) "The Universe Alone" from the *Paper Gods* album. It's an exquisite experience to sit outdoors under the stars with that song chiming in, then building into a crackling explosion of perfection.

I had the privilege of attending the concert at the Kennedy Space Center Rocket Garden in 2019 where the band opened with it under sparkling drones...and it was euphoric. I highly recommend imitating the experience while camping, taking a walk in the country, or sitting on the back porch recovering from summer's heat.

49. ITSISK

The band celebrated the Apollo 11 mission.

As mentioned in the to-do item above, DD performed at the Kennedy Space Center. They were selected to celebrate the 50th anniversary of the Apollo 11 Moon Landing mission, which was July 16, 2019. Joining them on stage were the Brevard Symphony Orchestra and the Joyful Noise Choir. The company Studio Drift programmed two hundred drones to fly in imitation of a murmuration of sparrows overhead and re-dock at the end of DD's "The Universe Alone." Among the DD faves they played that night, such as "Planet Earth" and "Anyone Out There," the band also covered The Police's "Walking on the Moon."

50. To Do

Hang the lyrics on your wall.

Many fans select "The Chauffeur," "Save a Prayer," or "Ordinary World" as their favorite DD song. Those are valid—and fabulous—songs to pick as your Number One. Whatever your fave is, Google the words (or get them from the liner notes) and have them printed up in a fancy way for wall art.

Personally, I did that the cheapest way possible and printed them out at home on a piece of resume paper. Then, I hung it in a decorative frame that was on sale at a craft store. (I selected "Keep Me in the Dark" by Arcadia.)

You might be more artistic than I and able to paint the lyrics on your wall. You might have an artistic friend who can create a montage of the lyrics with illustration on a large canvas. However you wish to interpret this item on the to-do list, go for it! You can have Simon's poetry on your wall.

51. ITSISK

This November Tuesday...

November's a good month for DD albums! *Seven and the Ragged Tiger* was released on November 21, 1983. *Arena* was released on November 12, 1984. Arcadia's *So Red the Rose* was released on November 18, 1985. *Notorious* was released a year later, on November 18, 1986, though there are sources who say it was also November 21, like the third album. *Decade* was released on November 15, 1989. *Red Carpet Massacre* was released on November 13, 2007.

52. To Do

Hang the lyrics around your neck.

Duranies have gotten creative artistically and now make jewelry. Do a quick search on Etsy, or any crafty direct-to-consumer platform, and you'll find talented artists who make jewelry with phrases from Simon's poetry to wear on pendants and charms on necklaces, bracelets, anklets, and even earrings. (That's in addition to the logo designs you can purchase from the band merch shop to proclaim your obsession when getting dressed up for a night on the town.)

53. ITSISK

You can find meaningful sorrow and mourning in Simon's lyrics.

There's a trio of songs Simon prepared when mourning some of his friends and colleagues. If you listen to "Do You Believe in Shame," "Michael You've Got a Lot to Answer For," and "Ordinary World," you'll hear a theme of grieving friends and loved ones while seeking a way to move forward without...

54. To Do

Join a Zoom.

Duranies know how to hang out, even when we can't be together in person. One superfan who has built an online hangout is Andrew Golub (who has also published a few fabulous DD-centric books of his own). Known around social media platforms as Durandy, he hosts an online meetup the first Saturday of each month at 1:00 p.m. EST for a few hours. It's affectionately called *Durandy's Den*. You can email Jennifer ahead of time for your invite at: contact@durandy.com.

55. ITSISK

All the Guitarists

Danse Macabre brings together all the DD guitarists on one album. In alphabetical order, Dom Brown, Warren Cuccurullo, Nile Rodgers, and Andy Taylor play on the album's total of thirteen tracks.

56. To Do

Binge videos.

It is absolutely acceptable to set aside a block of time to binge-watch every DD DVD you own, or to stream a few hours of their videos online. It's perfectly healthy and a great way to catch yourself randomly dancing through the house for a quick bathroom break or to refill your wine gla—I mean water bottle.

57. ITSISK

They lift their own lyrics.

When DD released the single for "Serious," it included a B-side titled "Yo Bad Azizi." While driving home from the music store in late 1990 (probably Thanksgiving break from college?), I read it to my mom and said, "That sounds like the line in 'Is There Something I Should Know.'" And that's exactly what it was. "You're about as easy as a nuclear war" became a rough and rockin' B-side. What other "lifted lyrics" have you found and enjoyed?

58. To Do

Binge mashups.

While there are some artists who don't appreciate their music being mixed or "mashed," the members of DD have seemed to embrace at least one other creative helping to promote their work. We can embrace it, too. In early 2024, a clever person on TikTok mashed DD's "Rio" with Black Sabbath's "Paranoid" and the result was fantastic.

Folks have been mashing DD's tracks for at least the past decade, with one amazing Clash-plus-Duran mix of "Rock the Casbah" and "Girls on Film" that will blow your mind if you're any kind of eighties fan.

Bands have been sampling DD tracks over the years, of course. I think everyone recognizes and gets excited about Notorious B.I.G. using "Notorious." Mark Ronson assisted Bruno Mars in sampling a bit of it into "Uptown Funk" as well. Australian-based band, 5 Seconds of Summer, sampled "Hungry Like the Wolf" in their 2016 song, "Hey Everybody!" They were even so kind as to give DD writing credit, even though 5 Seconds of Summer borrowed only the tune as opposed to the lyrics.

For this to-do item, I encourage exploring the mashups that smash two existing songs into one cohesive blend. It amazes me how artists can mix keys and time signatures into one another. This is a skill that impresses and pleases me greatly when it's done right. I highly recommend searching for "Duran Duran vs (insert band name)" and letting the sonic treasures unfold.

59. ITSISK

On your own in Tel Aviv...

Did you know there are lyrics to the instrumental that appears on the band's first album? When Simon was vacationing in Israel (some sources say he was volunteering on a kibbutz), he wrote out full lyrics for "Tel Aviv," which you can hear on the AIR Studio recording.*

The band played the instrumental version of the song live with the Orlando Philharmonic Orchestra on July 18, 2005, as part of the *Astronaut* tour. I'm pretty sure I had an out-of-body experience when the song began, having never expected to hear it live, much less with an entire orchestra supporting it!

**The AIR Studio recording of "Tel Aviv" is available to listen to on the band's official YouTube channel. You can also pick up the double-disc of the re-released first album and B-sides, and unreleased AIR Studio recordings of "Girls on Film" and "Tel Aviv," the Manchester Square demos of "Anyone Out There," "Planet Earth," "Friends of Mine," and "Late Bar," the BBC Radio 1 versions of "Night Boat," "Girls on Film," "Anyone Out There," and "Like An Angel," and the two different night versions of "Planet Earth" and "Girls on Film" from 2010 from EMI Records Ltd.*

60. To Do

Watch a Mulcahy film.

I'm not talking about "Planet Earth," "My Own Way," "Lonely in Your Nightmare," "Save a Prayer," "Hungry Like the Wolf," or "Rio." I recommend looking up Australian director and producer Russell Mulcahy's full-length movies for a Mulcahy binge. These include *Razorback* and *Highlander*—both from the 1980s—and *Resident Evil: Extinction*. If you're in the mood for a superhero movie, Russell directed *The Shadow*. You can find many more, including television series, from him if you're looking for it.

61. ITSISK

Where's John?

During March of 1997, the video for "Out of My Mind" dropped with its haunting, Victorian imagery. Online chat groups immediately buzzed with the question, "Where's John?"

Having experienced the emotional upheaval in the small audience at the convention where John announced he was leaving the band; I didn't have the heart to respond to these unsuspecting fans. Instead, I watched as others answered with the devastating news that John was no longer a part of the group. For many Duranies, the release of the "Out of My Mind" video was when they learned one of the founders they'd adored since the early eighties was exploring his own creative endeavors for a while.

62. To Do

Play for keeps.

In 1986, Atlantic Records included Arcadia's (the side project Simon, Nick, and Roger worked on) "Say the Word" on the soundtrack of the cheeky and poorly acted teen movie *Playing for Keeps*.

If you're in the mood to make up a drinking game or to have a campy film playing in the background at your next eighties party, watching that movie is an option. The song was lit, but the movie was disappointing (in this author's humble opinion).

63. ITSISK

The first album was released in 1981.

Duran Duran was the debut studio album, released on June 15, 1981, just five days before Bassist John Taylor's twenty-first birthday. How's that for a great birthday present? It was produced by Colin Thurston under the EMI label. (Please note, there is a version of the first album under the Harvest label.)

Capitol re-released *Duran Duran* during the spring of 1983 with a new cover design and the addition of "Is There Something I Should Know" in place of "To the Shore." (Personally, I think both would've served just fine on the album, but I'm not a record executive; I'm an author with an extreme bias toward both songs.)

64. To Do

Wrap it up.

It might not be easy to collect all the designs, but DD's merch shop has carried different varieties of DD wrapping paper.

In the event you can't find that posh item in which to wrap your Duranie friends' gifts, you can get crafty and make your own. In this day of free online graphic design programs—I'm thinking specifically of Canva—you can create something unique to make your friend's day when you hand them their next birthday present.

65. ITSISK

The second album was released in 1982.

Rio was the band's second album and was released on May 10, 1982. Again, the producer was Colin Thurston. And again, it was under the EMI label.

It's difficult to express how smug I feel seeing the continued success of that album and the continued accolades it receives during present day, considering the lukewarm-to-hostile reaction critics had for it back in the eighties. I'd like to imagine those critics grumbling their apologies to the fans, but that's more editorializing than is probably proper for this romp through Durandom.

66. To Do

Send a note.

Again, it might not be easy to find them all, but DD's merch shop has carried different sizes and themes of DD greeting cards.

In the event you can't find those posh items to send messages via snail mail to your Duranie friends, you can get crafty and make your own. Again, think of the myriad postcard and flyer services out there that help you design marketing materials. How easy would it be to take one of the many creative commons images of the band and design something you're not selling, but instead are using to make your friends smile?

67. ITSISK

The third album was released in 1983.

Seven and the Ragged Tiger was the band's third album and was released on November 21, 1983. That time, there were three producers listed. In alphabetical order, they are Duran Duran, Ian Little, and Alex Sadkin. It was released by EMI Capitol.

That is the album that introduced me to the band and began the obsession that has shaped my friendships, vacations, and musical stylings. If it weren't for a St. Louis deejay playing

"New Moon on Monday" one evening, would I have rushed to my friend Wendy to share "this cool song I heard last night" and be overwhelmed by her collection of DD books? Would I have started down that road?

68. To Do

Have your own Secret Oktober.

We already mentioned for one of the things you should know, DD is big on releasing albums during the month of November. It turns out, October's pretty good for them, as well, having released *Big Thing, Medazzaland, Future Past,* and *Danse Macabre* on Octobers 17 of 1988, 14 of 1997, 22 of 2021, and 27 of 2023, respectively. You can take advantage of this timing by playing those specific albums during the month of October. It's a great excuse to put them on repeat.

69. ITSISK

The fourth album was released in 1984.

Arena was the band's fourth album, although not recorded in a studio, and was released on November 12, 1984. The producers were Duran Duran and the fabulous Nile Rodgers. It was released under the Parlophone label.

70. To Do

Visit the star.

This is a to-do item you can control, depending on your vacation days and physical location. Visit the DD star on the Hollywood Walk of Fame. It's located in front of the Capitol Records building at 1770 Vine Street. (The ceremony for the DD star was held on August 23, 1993.)

71. ITSISK

The fifth album was released in 1986.*

Notorious was the band's fifth album and was released on November 18, 1986. The producers were Duran Duran and Nile Rodgers. The label was EMI Capitol.

**You'll see the band skipped a year getting Notorious out the door. We fans were concerned, not only because we had that extra year between Arena and Notorious, but also because The Power Station and Arcadia had released albums as splinter groups. Rumors of a break-up were going wild.*

72. To Do
Indulge

Eat some cherry ice cream.
Preferably with other Duranies.
While listening to *Rio*.

73. ITSISK
The sixth album was released in 1988.

Big Thing was the band's sixth album and was released on October 17, 1988. The producers were, in alphabetical order: Daniel Abraham, Duran Duran, Jonathan Elias. The label was EMI.

[And if you don't mind me editorializing for a moment, I believe the songs "Palomino" and "Land" are two of the most beautiful songs DD has crafted, along with "Wing," "Falling," "Save a Prayer," "Like an Angel," "My Antarctica," and the list could go on. My point is the second side of *Big Thing* is too often overlooked, and I highly recommend a re-listen anytime.]

74. To Do
Check it twice.

Make a list of all the slow, moody, atmospheric DD songs. Then rank them in the order of ones you love the most. I bet it will be impossible to select your top five, especially if you factor in Arcadia, but you might be able to pick your top ten.

75. ITSISK

The seventh album was released in 1989.

Decade was the band's seventh album and was released on November 15, 1989. It's a greatest hits record so it has all the producers. In alphabetical order, they are Daniel Abraham, Jason Corsaro, Duran Duran, Bernard Edwards, Jonathan Elias, Ian Little, Shep Pettibone, Nile Rodgers, Alex Sadkin, and Colin Thurston. It was released under the EMI label.

76. To Do

Do some side projects and solo research.

If you've been a Duranie for any length of time, you're probably aware of the side projects the band members participate in. It wasn't only the 1980s and 1990s that saw band members collaborating with other artists to create extra music that didn't quite fit into the DD sphere.

Use this to-do item to explore the magnificence of those side projects. Check out the beautiful symphonic instrumentals Nick has recently [2021] worked on with Wendy Bevan in the *Astronomia* Quartet. The four discs are distributed by Lege Artis Music.

If you want something eclectic, dig through Simon's Syn Music at www.syn.world. Or kick it old school and find an old copy of *Heaven's Eyes,* the remixes-rich addition to Arcadia's *So Red the Rose*.

Go back to the late nineties and review the Neurotic Outsiders' rippin' angst rock. Did you know The Power Station recorded a second album? Did you know John Taylor had a series of incredible solo albums, with one offering the stunning song "Immortal?"

I can't recommend this exercise highly enough to dive into the *extra* Duran.

77. ITSISK

The eighth album was released in 1990.

Liberty was the band's eighth album and was released on August 20, 1990. It was produced by Duran Duran and Chris Kimsey. The label was Parlophone.

78. To Do

Get high in Hollywood.

I swear I'm not condoning drug use.

Instead, I'm suggesting you gather up a group of Duranies and watch *A Hollywood High*, since it's now available on Blu-ray.

[Are you comfortable enough with my editorializing for me to share my experience in the theater? Because I live in a fairly small community, I drove an hour to the nearest Regal Cinema showing *A Hollywood High* when it was released around North America. Because I live far away from most of my Duranie friends, I went alone and met up with random strangers who love the band. We had a fabulous time singing along, dancing in our seats to keep the people in back from flipping out too badly, and just overall being in the moment. I encourage you to do that. At home. With a big-screen TV and no fussy people in the seats behind you.]

79. ITSISK

The ninth album was released in 1993.

Duran Duran—also known as *The Wedding Album*—was the band's ninth album, released on February 15, 1993. It was produced by Duran Duran and John Jones. The label was Parlophone.

80. To Do

Relax your pet peeve.

Do you have a specific pet peeve when it comes to the band or one of their songs? Does it get under your skin when a stranger asks, "Oh my God, are they still together?" Does it make you crazy when someone says, "I think three brothers growing up to be in the same band is so cool." Maybe it drives you nuts when an author tries to save space by abbreviating the band's name.

My personal pet peeve is when someone states the song title as "Hungry Like ***A*** Wolf." Typing that made my eye twitch. However, I have learned over the years to be calm and give grace when someone mis-speaks the title of a DD song. If you think about it, they're engaging in a conversation about our favorite band in a positive, excited, or curious way. I/we should be pleased to stoke their inquisitiveness and correct with kindness.

You can simply reply, "Yes, they've been together in one form or another since 1978."

"What's cool is all three Taylors came from different families and that's a bizarre coincidence."

And, in my case, I don't correct anyone for saying the title of a song incorrectly, because, in the long run, it doesn't matter. Unless they're writing it in a book...

81. ITSISK

The tenth album was released in 1995.

Thank You was the band's tenth album. It consisted of eleven covers plus a twelfth, re-imagined cover of "The Chauffeur" titled "Drive By," which, if listened to through noise-cancelling headphones in the dark, will overwhelm one's emotions. It was released on March 27, 1995. The producers were Duran Duran and John Jones. The label was Parlophone.

82. To Do

Get more than one.

Do you still have a CD player in your car? I have an older model vehicle with a CD player, and I dig that. This means I need *Rio* in the car, and I need *Rio* in the house. You see where I'm going with this, right? It's totally valid to have more than one copy of every album.

83. ITSISK

The eleventh album was released in 1997.

Medazzaland was the band's eleventh album, named after a dental hallucinogenic state, and released on October 14, 1997. The producers are an eclectic mix, including the company Nick Rhodes and Warren Cuccurullo had formed at the time, TV Mania, and the company Simon Le Bon, Yasmin Le Bon, and Nick Wood formed in 1991, Syn Productions. The label was Capitol.

84. To Do

Learn more about a wild boy.

In 2008, Andy Taylor wrote a memoir called *Wild Boy: My Life in Duran Duran*. That was just a few short years after he left the band for a second time. It was a decision that saddened many fans. In the book, Andy explores his life both pre and post DD. The book is available on Amazon and other online book retailers.

85. ITSISK

The twelfth album was released in 2000.

Pop Trash was the band's twelfth album and was released on June 19, 2000. The producers were TV Mania and Syn Productions. It was under the Hollywood label.

86. To Do

Watch and quote.

When was the last time you watched *Sing Blue Silver*? Is it time to sit down and relive your tweens? Maybe you're new to this DD obsessiveness and you've not seen the wacky delight. I encourage you to find a copy and enjoy it this weekend.

After watching (and re-watching) *Sing Blue Silver,* you probably have all those phrases we used to quote at each other running on a loop in your brain. [I mean, gimme a wrist band!] I challenge you to fit three or more of them into your day today. And, no, it won't be contrived; you can work them in seamlessly if you try.

87. ITSISK

The thirteenth album was released in 2004.

Astronaut. Finally.

Astronaut was the band's thirteenth album and was released on September 28, 2004, to a world of rabid Duranies. It signified the return of the full lineup as we remembered them. It was our youth restored in sonic form, and it was glorious. The producers were, in alphabetical order: Dallas Austin, Duran Duran, Don Gilmore, Nile Rodgers, and Mark Tinley. The label was Epic. As was the tour...

88. To Do

Cure boredom.

During 1995 and 1996, Nick Rhodes and Warren Cuccurullo recorded a sort of concept album called *Bored with Prozac and the Internet?* Because they were waiting for the perfect timing and Nick had misfiled the original tapes, the album was not released until March 11, 2013. Instead of regular, full-length songs, *Bored with Prozac and the Internet?* contained TV samples and looping tracks.

It tells the story of a family of four who are obsessed with new technology, among other things. It's a classic tale about individuals who sign their lives away to achieve fame. If you want to feed your esoteric Duranie side, then check out this album.

89. ITSISK

The fourteenth album was released in 2007.

That three-year gap made the fans nervous, and those fears were well-founded with the second departure of Andy Taylor.

Red Carpet Massacre was the band's fourteenth album and was released on November 13, 2007. The producers were an odd mix. In alphabetical order, they were Jim Beanz, Jimmy Douglass, Duran Duran, Nate "Danja" Hills, Timbaland, and Justin Timberlake. The label was Epic.

90. To Do

Listen to some Bowie.

As a true Duranie, it's good to visit the artists who have influenced the band. Along with David Bowie, you could play some Roxy Music, the Beatles, Genesis, Mick Ronson, AC/DC (Andy's contribution), Chic, and Siouxsie and the Banshees. Of course, there are many more, but that should get a good beginner's playlist going.

91. ITSISK

The fifteenth album was released in 2010.

All You Need Is Now was the band's fifteenth album and was released on December 21, 2010. The producers were Duran Duran and Mark Ronson. The label was Tape Modern.

92. To Do

Do they know it's Christmas?

While there were/are DD Christmas ornaments available from the band's merch shop, you can make your own DD-centric ornaments for your tree. You can play the Band-Aid "Do They Know It's Christmas?" song while you stitch DD lyrics about angels on your Christmas stocking. Whatever you find soothing for the season, here's your to-do item to augment your holiday cheer.

93. ITSISK

The sixteenth album was released in 2015.

Paper Gods was the band's sixteenth album and was released on September 11, 2015. The producers were Josh Blair, Duran Duran, Mr. Hudson, Nile Rodgers, and Mark Ronson. The label was Warner Bros.

94. To Do

Dress the part.

You don't necessarily have to wait for a date like Halloween to dress up as your favorite DD video character, although there are some—I'm looking at you, Iguana Dude from "Union of the Snake"—for which you might want a specific destination.

You'll get a mini thrill to thrift a beige, single-button, linen blazer with shoulder pads, distress it and push up the sleeves like a fellow who's running through a jungle marketplace on the hunt after you, add a tiger pendant necklace, and see who at the grocery store stops you in the cereal aisle to say, "You remind me of that fellow in that fabulous eighties video, the one about the wolf."

Now, you can get wildly creative if you're going to a DD convention or a Halloween party. My goodness. For something like that, you can do anything from becoming Barbarella to donning a *Danse Macabre* mask...if you don't mind.

95. ITSISK

The seventeenth album was released in 2021.

Future Past was the band's seventeenth album and was released on October 22, 2021. The producers were Erol Alkan, Joshua Blair, Duran Duran, and Giorgio Moroder. It included a host of fantastic artists, such as Bowie's Michael David Garson and Blur's Graham Coxon. The label was BMG Tape Modern.

96. To Do

Celebrate a Duraniversary.

Do you remember the first time you had a slumber party with friends, and you stayed up most of the night watching DD videos and playing the *Into the Arena* boardgame? Maybe you have the ticket stub from your first DD concert, so you know the *exact* date to celebrate. This is your permission to revive a lost tradition of getting together with friends or calling a fellow Duranie who lives far away to celebrate an anniversary.

One-year, twenty-five-year, or a random number that means nothing to anyone but you—take this opportunity to reach out to someone and relive a DD memory together. Set up a DD "lunch date" where you listen to songs from your DD playlist. If you're at work, maybe you do this through your earbuds, so you don't disturb co-workers. If you work from home, you can do this however you wish, letting the music envelop you as you dive into your food. Let your Duraniversary lunch nourish body and soul!

97. ITSISK

The eighteenth album was released in 2023.

Danse Macabre was the band's eighteenth album, consisting mostly of covers the band felt contributed nicely to a Halloween theme. They also "covered" three of their own songs ("Nightboat," "Love Voudou," and "Secret Oktober 31st"), included three original songs ("Black Moonlight," the title track, and "Confession in the Afterlife"), and released it on October 27, 2023 (Simon's birthday). The producers were Josh Blair, Duran Duran, Mr. Hudson, and Nile Rodgers. The label was BMG Tape Modern.

98. To Do

Go see a cover band.

DD has inspired musicians to take to the stage in their honor. Not only did fifteen bands come together to cover DD songs on a complete tribute album released in October 1997, but bands have formed for the purpose of "playing tribute" on a regular basis. One such band is Tiger Tiger, which you can see if you make a trip to the United States' West Coast.

99. ITSISK

At long last!

After many years of fans petitioning to further honor their favorite band, DD was inducted into the Rock & Roll Hall of Fame in November 2022.

100. To Do

Let Them Know.

Finally, the one-hundredth thing for a DD fan to know or do during this life is to write a fan letter to their favorite member of the band.

Doesn't that sound easy? Way back in the day, there were addresses printed in the classified sections of magazines like *Smash Hits*, *Bop!*, and *Right On* that helped you get a fan letter to a band's "headquarters" or managers.

Nowadays, you can find band members on different social media platforms, hanging out in chat groups, or hosting (or being hosted in) livestream events. There are ways to reach out and let a celebrity know how he or she has influenced or inspired you. I encourage you to let the guys know.

To communicate directly with DD, you send an email to their assistant, Katy Krassner: askkaty@duranduran.com.

For example, about fifteen years ago, when I was near death thanks to some funky treatments for cancer and the hospital's not-socompetent handling of my side effects, I wanted to let John Taylor know his band had provided a wonderful and meaningful soundtrack to my life. I didn't go into the fact I was weak and unable to swallow food or water; that wasn't the point. The point was to let the fellow who had influenced and inspired me for about twenty-five years at the time know a fan in Florida was thankful for the music.

Don't we all love it when someone recognizes the work we've put into our dreams? It's similar to leaving a review on a book's Amazon or Barnes & Noble listing. It's a feel-good way to spread positivity and joyfulness into the universe. Your fan letter is good for your soul, as well as that of the person receiving it. I highly recommend the exercise not only to send out a jolt of optimism and goodwill for a member of the band, but also to give yourself the adrenaline rush of positivity.

If DD has influenced you in useful ways, if they've given you a song that's helped you through a tough time, if they've facilitated awesome friendships or trips with lifelong BFFs to cities to hang out and see a show, let them know. Open up an email window and write what's in your heart. Your heart will thank you...as I thank you, my reader, for spending time reflecting on these one hundred quirky, frivolous items of random DD fun.

Afterword

This note is for new Duranie friends of mine. Thank you for reading this quick, quirky guide to fun elements that make a DD fan tick. In case the past fifty pages didn't convince you of it, I've found amazing inspiration in the music and presence of the band.

More than one hero I've written over the years has been inspired by members of the band. An obvious one is spelled out in the introduction to my 2015 release, *May Your Heart Be Light*, the first in my vampire-satire series.

I share, in December 2006, I was experiencing a tumultuous point in my adult life and the closest DD friend couldn't get time off work to accompany me on a ten-hour drive to Atlanta for the meet-n-greet John Taylor was holding in support of his new bass guitar and clothing line launch at Macy's. So, I drove up there alone. It was one of the best decisions I've made in life.

Hanging out with other fans during a remarkably low point in my life was good for my mental health. Meeting the kind and personable Mr. Taylor amid others who were also excited to be in the line of fans was exactly the medicine I needed.

On the ten-hour drive home (with a short nap at a truck stop somewhere in North Florida), I dreamed up a story about a debonair, kindly vampire. He owns a bed-and-breakfast in Colorado, and he survives because of the friends around him.

More than my heroes have been inspired by the band. If you pick up the *Choices* epic fantasy series, the instances of DD inspiration will fully entertain the clued-in Duranie yet be invisible to non-fans. It's standard for radio hosts, journalists, bloggers, podcasters, and others to ask authors what inspires us. I often answer with "music," because that's true.

But if we want to get technically correct, Duran Duran has been, is, and will forever be an inspiration for my creative ventures. This obsession is fun, silly at times, hopeful at others, inspirational always, and a means to meeting friends who have joined me on a long and meaningful musical road.

I'm so pleased to now count you among Duranie friends of mine. I hope you find amusement and continuing joy in some of the activities from this book. One of the easiest ways to share your inspirational moments "around" this book is on social media. I have an active Twitter account (@SandyLender) and a YouTube channel called @SandySaysRead where I tend to talk about books. Please chime in there! And, of course, you can share your DD thoughts and stories within a review of this book on Amazon, Goodreads, or wherever fine books are discussed online.

I look forward to chatting with you out there or at the next DD show!

(Below: Roger, Jennine, Simon, John, Sandy, Nick before a concert in 2008)

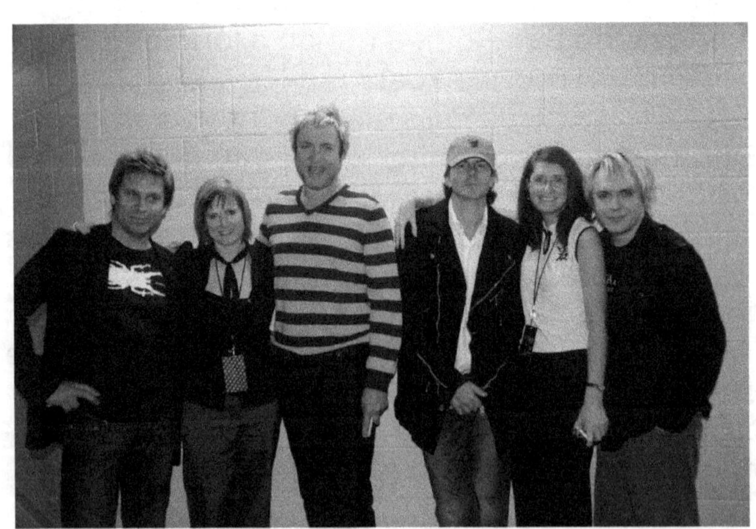

About the Author

Fantasy Author Sandy Lender is an international best-selling poet and an award-winning author for her fantasy, literary fiction, poetry, and short story works.

Sandy is a construction magazine editor by day and author of #GirlPower fantasy novels by night living in Florida to help with sea turtle conservation and parrot rescue. You can follow her author page on Amazon (Sandy Lender) or subscribe to her free SandySaysRead newsletter (bit.ly/SSReNews) to stay up to date.

With a four-year degree in English and thirty-year career in publishing, Sandy's successes include traditionally and self-published novels, hundreds of magazine articles, multiple short stories in competitive anthologies, a handful of technical writing awards, a handful of creative writing awards, and the 2023 Michael Knost Wings award.

Sandy's been writing stories since she was knee-high to a grasshopper when her great-grandmother shared her odd little tales of squeaky ghost-spiders around an apartment complex in Southern Illinois. The stories have developed to include strong young ladies working with dragons to save worlds from terrible fates, but those pesky spiders still show up from time to time.

There's always something brewing at Sandy Lender Ink headquarters where *some days, you just want the dragon to win.*

SandyLenderInk.com

www.ingramcontent.com/pod-product-compliance
Lightning Source LLC
LaVergne TN
LVHW010542100826
845148LV00013B/2567

* 9 7 8 1 7 3 7 8 1 2 9 6 8 *